SARAH PRITCHARD

WHEN WOMEN FLY
(THE SEVEN AGES
OF A MAD WOMAN)

Published in 2019
Hidden Voice Publishing
www.hiddenvoicepublishing.co.uk

Cover Art By: Cwtch Jones
Enquiries: dljones63@hotmail.com

MRS. PUTNAM, *glancing at Betty:* How high did she fly, how high?

PARRIS: No, no, she never flew—

MRS. PUTNAM, *very pleased with it:* Why, it's sure she did. Mr. Collins saw her goin' over Ingersoll's barn, and come down light as a bird, he says! (I.75-77)

The Crucible Arthur Miller

We all have wings

But some of us don't know why…

From 'Never Tear Us Apart' INXS/Paloma Faith

Dedicated to:

Rachel Cook, Jan Freeman & Kimberley Waller,
who flew away too soon &
the other mothers in the sky.

CONTENTS

WHEN WOMEN FLY
THE SEVEN AGES OF A MAD WOMAN

IV. BLUE STOCKING PRO

V. BARREN MADONNA

VI. GRAND MOTHER WITCH

VII. WISE CRONE

WHEN WOMEN FLY

FORWARD FORWARD FORWARD

WHEN WOMEN FLY...

SEE ME FLY
Lil ol' Bastard love child from everywhere,
military baby, outside of marriage,
given up for adoption, got back,
adopted by step father
only child to continue in His name...

I have always been the daughter of a witch
& a bitch & a whore.
Damned if I did &
Damned if I didn't
So I did

Fly in the face of patriarchy, hypocrisy,
divide n rule school for fools,
sexism, homophobia,
xenophobic unloves
calling me a wyrd sistah
I'll take it.

Still wanting a piece of me
the flesh of my spirit is not for sale
to any religion or institutional rhetoric
No monopoly or capitalising
of My wings.

I stir up potions & lotions in the cauldron
of the wild
I am my own freedom fighting soul
flown, high, high & oh so low low

from deep, dark blue waves to dangerous pink
khaki camouflage
sunsets.

I reroute, regroup, retroupe,
shape shift tribe by tribe
blue birds, Camp Fire Girls
The Runts, the verruccas
Sunday Girls, pretty disgusting things
The Outlanders, Batty Smiths,
Panic Street Teachers, 3 Muses
the peacocks Poetry Lovers Out Loud,
from broken pieces, english Alien, space2Bnatural.co.uk
I have always been an outsider wounded healer
a child of domestic violence
waving the flag of peace at
the tank of Mr. Big
saying 'it's me Daddy, it's me!'
Hoping for a Star Wars Bar of diversity
without the wars.

because the world is a better place with the whole world in it
& why wait to die to
Rest in Peace?
Horse feathers hold me high.
Let us flock & rock
this lil blue dot
in a circle of our wings
back to the shine of shades of green & peaceful times.

Everyday saints risen from crosses of
oppression, suppression, depression,
Let us fire up in EXPRESSION

singing from the same heretic hymn sheet.
See us fly

(from this witch's pulpit)

I. BASTARD LOVE CHILD

HIGH HORSES

I am flying high as a wild woman
a 9 year old scientist, explorer galloping
on my Palomino, Shetland, Apache pony.
I am the Lone Ranger
test tube in hand
eagle-eyeing for arrow heads
along the banks of The Ohio!

My Pegasus canons me through the air
I taste the stony earth
she returns, over me
her blue glass eyes
staring down through her blond mane
at the precocious blond brat
that left her an ocean away.

I design pine shelves for every kind of model horse
a cavalry of wise heads above me;
cloth, metal, pottery, metal, plastic, straw
from countries passed through and wished for
a parade of all my animal dreams.
I am the blue faced Boudica from East Anglia
charging back at the Imperial Roman invaders
I hold horse power in the palm of my hand.

Now I look across a desk,
down a corridor of doors

through a window to clouds of white horses racing to me.
I am an unwilling Trojan horse in an alien territory,
a sea horse swimming against the tide.
I flick and kick as good as any mare
I rear & tear at the constraints of Man
I'm stomping on the floor
bucking at the crowds
looking for other wide open spirited eyes.
I'm heading for the hills
stampeding for freedom.

GIVE AWAY CHILD

I was one of those children
that Mums give away
and ask for back.
I am already growing up
in separate places.

I cry in The Home
my mother cries for days.
He paces the small front room
Nana tells him to go get me back.

One side of my face
did not grow
and I cannot have breast now.
We are both punished.

The oversize pram
Nana bought to celebrate
big, shiny, taxi cab black
is too big for a car or pavement.
We walk everywhere in fresh air.

I am left outside Woolies.
She's at home
remembering she's forgotten something.
Nobody steals me. We clear the pavements
speeding home.

I travel the size
of her handbag
the size of her suitcase
the size of Nana's pram
across the world
following her following her men.

SKIN BETRAYED

'my skin has betrayed me…
Moma's in the bedroom with
The door closed.' Audre Lorde

I can hear noises I do not want
to hear, he is a bear & she is a faun
he is flinging and pouncing on &
I am under the bedclothes
cuddling my kitten
and scratching out the noises.

Moma's taking me to school
She is trying on different clothes
until he likes the colour
likes the feel, likes the shape
over her Mummy body
and she is coming out of the door in her high
heels the way he likes her
I am sitting in the back seat
cuddling my monkey toy
and scratching out the noises.

Moma's trying to get the house ready
for the party and
they disagree on where the glasses go
and where the clock should tick
and they are flying across the room

and I am rocking on the elephant stool
scratching out the noises.

SCAR FACE

Grady is my six year old boy friend
cos ever'body says so,
so we walk to school holding hands.
And I have to wear a gold coloured heart
locket with his face in
I don't like.

I'd rather investigate
the big spider cactus
and see if I can figure out how
to touch them without getting stabbed
so that when lost in the desert
I can drink them.
But my hand is still in Grady's
and it's hard to walk
bumpin' all over.

We see the bad boys comin'
along the white sandy alleys
between other people's houses we walk.
Grady froze, so I had to too
and then they ran at us
and threw hard the big log
in my face.
Grady is shakin'.
He pulls my hand that is not on my bloody face
until we are at his house.

His father gives me to his Mom
to wash my face.
I have long, red scratches.
I might have scars like sword marks.
Grady's Dad takes Grady's hand
into another room.
I know he has taken his belt off.
I hear him belt Grady
because he didn't save me-
And WHAT will my Mom say
when she comes home from hospital
all sad after giving away her baby
and sees my face?

INVISIBLE BROTHER

Mom said it was like
giving a puppy to a new home
when she had to go into
hospital to have a baby
to give to a good home.
It was a boy we call George now.
Mom also said we couldn't keep him
because if my first Dad found out
he might stop Mom keeping me
because she had been BAD
having a baby without him.
He'd say she was an unfit Mom
for me.
Mom said she wanted George to go to
a Christian home
and thinks he went to New England
which is funny cos we're from England.

When Mom left the hospital
without George
a black nurse called after her
to tell her
'Ma'am you've left your baby.'
She didn't know it was on purpose
and Mom's mouth was full of tears
so she could not speak and had to keep walking
to pick me up from friends

where I had a bloody face from the bullies
and she cried, so I cried.
Even though she explained it all
I still wanted a new baby.

It is funny how
George was like me, a mistake
but he had to be given away
so I got to stay.
Maybe they'll get him back
one day, like they did with me.
Later I find out my first Dad
did know about George and signed the papers
to give George away and my second Dad
also knew about George but
two children that were not his own were
too much.

All these things are jigsaw pieces
I put back together
to see a better picture.

I am sorry George, I couldn't save you
and I never saw you or held you
or even said good bye.
You are a frozen boy
in the shadow of my heart.
You pop up when I am not ready
and stick in my throat & eyes.

You get bigger just behind me.
You haunt Mom
and jerk her head with sobbing
for all your uncelebrated birthdays.

You are our beautiful, mysterious,
Florida son, brother,
our lost sunshine boy.
Perhaps you will find
the pieces that are us
One day.

MY MUSEUM

I am a bright American, blond brat.
I am eleven and I have been returned to England
where I was born a long time ago.
I am digging in the earth
in the corner of our buildings
where years of rubbish
from Nana's farm lie.
I line up old cog wheels of broken machines,
a bright blue spode chip,
a Wilson's snuff tin,
a big, bent old penny.
In the old hay loft I save
our thrown away parts.

Mother learned to drive when she was twelve
on a tractor in the field
with the leathery old men
who patted her on the backside
like a fine young filly.
GramPapa knew every inch of the fields in the village.
Mother helped harvest, watch the rabbits out run the combine
bindatwine belted men and balers.
Uncle Coddy with his missing fingers
seasoned to obey the land.

Every Sunday Nana puts out

the Spode for high tea
with salmon and cucumber sandwiches
and bowl like cups of tea
with blue trees, blue bridge, blue pagoda, blue people
and a blue bird.
Nana married the skeletal faced man in the grey picture
by Neptune's temple, Cairo.
From Surrey she sent my mother and her sister
to Norfolk full of flying Stars and Stripes men,
while she works on Hawker Siddeley Rolls-Royce plane
engines.
He is killed by mistake, by a British plane.
Was it blue?

Grandpapa takes snuff
In a pinch on the dip of his left hand
sniffed into his large hairy nostrils
and later sneezed into his browned hankies.
He offers it to me and I proudly try.
I think I am going to die or

my head explode out of the red
pick-up truck we deliver wood in.
I have no hanky to catch it in.
He teaches me to scythe & chop kindling wood
like the son he didn't have
And how to carry heavy bags like my mother did.

I dig through Nana's desk

when the house is quiet.
I find her small case full of huge old pennies
and an envelope with an American stamp on.
It's a letter from my U.S.A.F. father.
I try to write to the address and ask what he's like?
Nana whispers to my mother who whispers to me
'He was never your real father you know.'
I remember him throwing Aunty Kath's
big old clock at my mother and shout, shouting.
'Good,' I think 'I'm not related to that,
and what makes a father real?'

In the old hay loft I play
with my twelve year old mother
my newly married Nana
and my peppery, wooden old Grandpapa.
We have all just finished the harvest.
We sip blue Spode tea
and sniff snuff.

II. DADDY'S MINX GIRL

PRIVATE NAMES

Glad to hear
your toddler has moved beyond
your careful debate
between the willy versus the fanny
onto forging her own names
for her private parts
'bumpers' and all!

SAD to know
her words
for her most precious places
will become eroded, corrupted
by a taboo list
of glossy pubescent mag-tags
and soft porn problem pages
and hard core heavy metal sages
and ill-conceived sex education
even though her fragile spaces
are still top of the possession list.

MAD to see
her words of childhood celebration
turn to shapes of squirm and flinch & degradation
where joy once sang.
But
one day a rhythm soft & warm will begin
to tap away inside

to a voice within that
whispers on irrepressible and
on another sleepless night
she will pick up a pen and

PAD to write
her drowned words back out
in testament, in witness, in memorial
of the little girl who grows and grows up & up
to still need her own words
for her own parts
to celebrate again and again
The Wonder of Her.

SHOOT! MAN!

The Lovett boys have a b-b gun.
We gather at the top of the gravel drive hill
where it swoops down through the trees.
We stand on look out.
I am always an Indian becos'
I am a girl.
I know I can shoot good as any cow boy even at nine.
I don't remember getting the gun.
I see the trees along the barrel,
no kick back, no sound of glass shattering
just the sharp punch
of three big breaths backwards
and a man in an estate wagon
who climbs back up the hill to us.
I don't know how
but I shot a man
in the back of the neck
They said.
He told on me and now

I am BAD.

My Mom gave me a thick lip
and a bloody nose
that drained into a cup
while Aunt sat rocking
like an old porch chair

not knowing what to do.
The man shot in the neck
-surprised at Mother's
apologetic English accent-
disappeared like the Lovett boys.
Shoot! Dang! Sons of guns!
I still can't figure out
how it ricocheted off the tree
through the back of his pick-up
into his red neck.
Man! What a cissie!

FAIRY GOD-DAUGHTER

You came visiting us in a flap
spitting feathers
looking like you were freshly plucked
with blue fin-like hands
conducting the air waves,
bruised from the battle to arrive
paddling frog-like through tears.

You left your pirate's mark
upon your mother
reeling grey and yellow
on swollen, water legs
she could barely remember how to use.
You simply tug and pluck
for more of her body
and your blessed bones
reach out greedily
giving us all a chance
to move to your wild, new dance
to the songs of a love child.

Daddy holds his dolly
to his chest
mother plays
with a soft toy March hare
and a parade of giants call
filling the room like a vase.

We pay homage
to your tiny and raw beauty
as our futures fly by
it is you who holds us.

NOT A GIRL YET

I swing backwards off metal railings
by the back of my knees
head inches above the concrete
and roller skate or go-cart
down a car-lined hill
and make for a gap in the corner
or scooter
after my mother's Beetle
away from the *au pair*
who couldn't stop me
from playing with matches
or take on the bully who ran me over
with his bike
or bite the backs of other boys
I don't like the look of
or swim to the raft in the lake
with snakes underneath
and try to rock everyone else off
or dive off the highest diving board
because my cousin was too scared to
and climb and climb and climb
to the tops of trees & roof tops & rocky look-outs.

And now my hips are exploding
and my chest is budding
and my father says
I'm sitting on a gold mine

and there are girls
who are not boys any more
who wear shirts all summer
and have come down from the trees
and away from me and the other boys
and sit in shadows glowering at a distance
and read books and books and books
whole collections of pages with no pictures
and I know I am not a girl yet
because I still feel my eyeball
rolling across the words heavily
and I still can't reach the end of the story
because my pockets are full of swapsies
and better things to do
and Patty says there are arrowheads
down by the bull frog pond
where we found the neat rabbit skeleton
hanging in the bush up-side-down,
so Patty's not a girl yet either I guess.

III. NUBILE LEZZIE

HOW DARE YOU

I have told my mother I prefer women
and introduced my lover to my father
I explained to my sisters why I have no boyfriend.
I have tormented myself through a year-long affair at school,
only to tell friends later who never guessed
and now I reprimand pupils for anti-gay slogans.
I have challenged my bosses' queer-bashing laughter
and had an affair with a woman
only four years younger than my mother.
On stage I have declared my tendencies
riddled out my inclinations in poems, jokes and cabaret.
In public I have worn the badges, sung the songs
and kissed the forbidden.
I have discussed The Color Purple with a nun at school,
speculated on the lesbian behaviour
of my tortoiseshell cat
and advertised a lesbian room.
Happily I have perpetuated our collective madness
until I came to you.
We have grown very close with all this bloody telepathy
your approval or rejection teetering on that knife edge
so powerful I have swallowed twenty-seven years of
personal progress.
How dare you tongue-tie me you smug, celibate temptress.

BREAST

You showed where your breast had been
I wanted to see a pink star
or a medical pattern
But instead I saw your womanhood hacked at.
You said you had always had young girl's breasts &
I wanted to weep in a megaphone
for you & the possibility of the poison in us all.
You walk tall & straight no less of yourself
& I pray it won't keep you from hugs & lovers
Most death-defying trait
to live even now
as if forever.

HER PENIS

(After Frieda Kahlo exhibition San Francisco 2008)

There's a woman with a penis
lying between her legs
a clitoris three inches long
flying beneath her
an indicator, antennae, unseen.
Reading unconnected she rises
watching, waiting, wanting
heat, moisture, rhythm.
On the settee in gentle conversation
on the bus
across the city
she is reminded of her urgency
to connect with futures
even if only ever with her eyes
over a drink
a new hand shake
a familiar cheek to kiss
shoulder and arms to envelop
her Venus point of pleasure
will rise and fall alongside her
a sensuous censor.

RAINBOW NATION

It comes through the radio
the Nation that calls itself Rainbow
traces the path of Paska
disappeared from her dancing friends
found in a field days later
family recognised only
from her leg tattoo.
Here such women are
raped to put them straight.
'if you package shit- it still smells the same'
quotes the homophobe.
No home here
rainbow sister
with the blue birds
over the rainbow now.

WHEN I DRINK YOU

Cherries and full blooded red berries
pickling in smokey oak with
a long lingering spicy after taste.
When I drink you I
get down on my
knees with the thrill of
You.
Come over, right here, right now.
Is it me or is it hotter in here
than the undergrowth of a jungle?
Dazzling and full of charm
as you are I cannot tell you
how fucking good you look
how you floor me because
I am at heart
a big fucking coward if
I say what drips from my lips
you will just fucking disappear
as quickly as the
full-bodied bottle of
red blood wine I
drink too quickly to
blur the edges.

OMNILOVE

when we have replaced my eyes
that saw you skeweredly
and my murmuring heart that
missed one too many beats
and given me more sensitive hands
to place on your metal heart beat as you
reach to place your plastic hand on my
metal heart beat
and our digital eyes do that miracle anew
of falling in love with each other
in synchronicity
when we have gone all around the planets
and returned to the mother ship again
when the ticking of loves past
quantum leap to here again
when we virtually wrap thighs around thighs
and forget what gender we are
and in artificial ignorance grope like aliens
towards unalgorithmically coded wave lengths
when we touch again
will you recognise me?

GUITAR WOMAN

You sent me to learn the guitar
because I was the son you didn't have
to copy Grandfather's way.
I played it until I let it go
rebelling the wrong way round.

But the woman playing a guitar
still struck chords in me that
resounded me into a first kiss
with another woman who said we stood
with our arms like
we were playing guitars.

The metronome is ticking right now
counting me down…3…2…1…
how many more heart beats before
I pick up the woman shaped instrument
to make music again?

THE LESBIAN IN US
(homage to Adrienne Rich)

She took me by the left hand
with her sinister wisdom
just when I needed an elder
wayward, Sapphic woman
to reassure me the love I
could not name did have a
common language, that
love between women wherever you
draw the skin-thin-line-between
is ok.
My tongue has twisted itself into a knot
to self-define that pleasure my first
woman lover gave me and years of crushes
and you with your poetry and magazine and
radical pamphlet blew away the hurled hate
words with your reasonableness birthing
heteronormative and compulsive
heterosexuality lifting the language trap
straight jacket I was eunuched in-
claimed, named and re-aimed our potency
that bore more fluid, growing more non-binaried
and more poetic by the day
making our own language tools, decolonising
the colonist's geography of woman with woman.
Gentler shoulders than Atlas held my world up
and even though I have chosen a mostly spinsterly path

I think of you whenever a woman looks at
another woman with pure love in her smile.

FRAGILE FREEDOM

Why do you have to ram it down our throats?
Why isn't there a straight PRIDE?
Yes, at times my pride
gets a lil frayed round the edges
another gay marriage debate headline
I who've managed to avoid children and marriage
but not the pain of a gay divorce
I who has wet dreams
of an LGBT friendly eco pod on sea
I who hold dear this delicate, finely-tuned
endangered species called
Freedom.

Why do you have to ram it down our throats?
Why isn't there a straight PRIDE?
Yes, I can do internalised homophobia too
I laugh at the feathers & leathers,
the flexi-sexy, the rubber, the latex, the sequins, the bears,
the sisters of indulgence in wimples & beards
All our super powered, all singing, all dancing dare.
Then I remember you messaged me
about being chased by hunters in Moscow
how they haunted and raped you
& left their trademark hate mark on your skin with a knife.
I look again at this precious finely-tuned endangered species
this fragile freedom you don't have.

Why do you have to ram it down our throats?
Why isn't there a straight PRIDE?
Yes even I can do homophobia inside & out
cringe at the merry-go-round of gay life
the Shane graphs, the shrinking pool of others my age
then I get your email
needing some support
while torn away from your family
and motherland.
You seek asylum here
and need pics of our march
with my dog & the gay flag
To prove how gay you are to the Home Office.
I look again at this precious, finely-tuned endangered
species called freedom and
I take up my tattered flag and
fly it high again.

IV. BLUE STOCKING PRO

CHEMICAL SUNSET

This the place I was reborn
in a red brick student population explosion
where they talk like a question mark
warmly wrapping my southern snatches
get Freudian to phallic horizons
or ecclesiastical aspirations
industrial exhaust pipes and towering blocks
from the cradle of blue hills to the breast of Old Central
and the wrought iron O of The Refuge
stone women hold up the city.

On University road children push rag dolls in prams
calling 'penny for the guy' or fags or whatever
a woman with a baby holds a polystyrene cup
for the price of a cuppa tea
her husband gambles says the Eighth Day worker
most mornings a high speed tea cosy
bombs away from my door
clutching band posters ironed straight for her bed
graffiti mouthed with varicose tights and laddered legs
she warns me I might never belong –
I'm a resident outsider, a transient inside.
At the car park to The Aaban films
knee-high toothless boys offer to guard
our old bangers for a price, from them.
Low status dressers and other fashion gurus
cat walk the Polytechnicolour avenues

exchange old records for new,
buy new-to-you clothes
have a bean feast, play spot the difference
the girls look blue, the boys are in the pink.

Watch her play at The Royal Northern College of Musical
culture vultures
catch a bus to make love to yourself
in the cockroach crescent with a concrete award
a futuristic Bath versus terraced times
lifts for coffins, stairwells for bogs, walls for angry messages
rubbish chutes for fire bombs, pavements for fouling
No Ball Games! allowed so turn the music louder
boys kick cans in condom car park
while black girls hug huge white plastic baby dolls
and the stray dogs rut on
against another glorious chemical sunset.
I am stared through by a thousand light-bulbed spectacles
danced with by a cast of shadows
and still the city is not big enough for all my lives
it passes me by like so many trains
I have always been good at missing
and the country calls back betrayal.

DEAR VIRGINIA

Five hundred guineas and a room of one's own?
No, Virginia much more.
Even allowing for inflation
even acknowledging historical perspective
even if we could ignore parental script
or hands that slip unwanted up skirts
or somehow
coexist with patriarchy
or Goddesses forbid create
a born-again matriarchy

Even if one had money enough
or even a house of one's own
or a garden that Vita envied
or we conquered slugs
even if we had a press of one's own
or should poetry become more popular than novels
even if -ist and -ism and -ology were redundant from our
language

Even if we saw the death of wars - not loved ones
still and surely Virginia
your stony pockets and watery grave
tell us so much more-
what a woman most needs Virginia,
without justification or apology is
A Mind Of One's Own.

GRASS ROOTS

Off Piccadilly Gardens down
campaign postered stair well
eventings, marches
into the cellar down
walls freshly
screen printed slogan tee-shirts
into the labyrinth of
books on grass roots politics that
fed me for years of my
toddler feminist adventures in Manchester pre-
internet and smart phones here
was the hub of what was happening left wingly
politicing in Revolution City…

Manchester Women's Liberation Newsletter,
Amazon Press across the road for small press
leaflets and novels and rooms to rent
in right-on shared houses
and where-to-get tickets to Greenham, the anti-Apartheid,
Anti-violence against Women, anti-nuclear,
Reclaim the Night, Anti-clause 28 demo-march, sit-in, civil
disobedience camp from Piccadilly Gardens to Burton
Woods. Readings by backstreet poets and lesbian nuns
breaking their silence
or red climbers, gardeners, cooks, plumbers
or pee in the unisex loo with the squidgy loo seat
listen to marginalised musicians or even

buy a book on My Body, My Self, socio-feminist
separatist manifestoes and the Peace Union song book.
Catch the eye of a like-minded alternatives, ask for
everything from
the wise being bookkeepers.
Come into the shadows together below
the shopping frenzies once
a week in sanctuary from
counselling in red
light pre-Village Bloom Street to
Earth myself.

NAMING ME

Pric Hard the children chanted down the corridor
I looked at my name
Pritchard- son of Richard
Looked at my mother's name-
Manley- Man like?
Looked at my grandmother's name
Johnson- son of John's town
Looked at my next great-great-mother
Mc Knight- kin of fighting man, great mother
Nelson- another boy child
Looked at my next great
Looked at her mother's again.
Corkhill?
The twisting hill she stood on.
I smiled and said my new name to myself
And sent the script off.
When another envelope arrived
I did not recognize my new self
addressed as
Cockhill.

V. BARREN MADONNA

WINTER BEACH

Unfolding unto the February sands
we walked once more our favourite edge
along the wash line collecting
beautiful stones.
I found a chalky three-holer
to add to my garden necklace
and the remains of a brick worn round
returning to its clay banks
washed in from the drowned cliff village.
Shipden houses the water people
mythologised by a low tide summer toll
of its resounding church bell
once doubled as a lighthouse.
You collect kelp and cuttle fish
and we argue over the possible uses
of a washed up lobster pot.
At the stone barrier the dogs run free
my pockets are full once more of this watery spree.
I chalk your name with 'I love-' in front…
It must be embarrassing to be my mother.
We are playing as we did 25 years ago.
I am in no hurry
to return to our separate homes
and opposing systems
trying to cope with our tides
of erosive sway-
all too often we wear each other down

wring each other to salt water
and forget what we leave behind.

SKELETON TREE

Our roots wandered restless, driven, drawn.
No cosy copse or orchard grew
where our seed scattered and blew.
Scotland, Ireland, Isle of Man, England
Liverpool, London, Norfolk, U.S.A.

A tall spinster aunt in white gloves and carriage,
red-haired mother cajoling bumptious children,
a boy chasing a kipper down a rain-filled gutter home,
a little girl delivering cakes with licked off icing,
a father who drove a Liverpool tug boat,
a young mother building bomber plane engines,
a young father hugging a gun instead of young daughters.
Victorian, war torn Great, and Grand parents
my roots, my bedrock, my backward flesh and blood.

We rattle our bony secrets at each other
ghostly figures dance round my unmade grave
'Make it better!', 'Make it better!'
But this tree has no living grandparents,
has three run away fathers,
has powerful mothers who live like witches in ruins
with goat, sheep and hounds
strirring her own ever stranger potions of love.

But this tree is good at losing men,
grandfathers dead before grandchildren born

fathers an ocean away
brother adopted
husband unmet
son unmade.
This tree bears female fruit
aunts, sisters, nieces and daughters in threes
who climb trees.

My night's eyes see
the hands of the clock of my ancestors
push, pull, point me forward.
but these broken branches,
that flown seed,
this rotten apple
will need more
than my humble gardening
to cure the twisted tree.

CHILD BLESSED
(after Billie Holiday)

Bless the boy whose father gives him
a condom for his 11th Christmas
whose mother gives him
a tin of lager for his 12th birthday
whose parents encourage him to become
a porn star.

Bless the child whose mother is beaten
whose father is a time bomb of a control freak
who lives with Nan and never sees Mum
whose parents gas themselves in a car
down a lonely lane one night.

Bless the child who doesn't remember
her mother's name
and never met his father
who fixes meals & washes her Gran in the morning
who she shares her bedroom with
then sorts her younger siblings.

Bless the child that goes through all this
before school, hears the whispers
catches the tone of stone heavy words
tossed across roads,
over lunch breaks, on toilet walls
that repeat the abuse.

Bless the child that has escaped Bosnia
in the month of daffodils
to run with his mother
to a foreign land who has
to twist his tongue
round a labyrinth of obstacles
to earn life's basic needs….

Bless the child that makes another child
before she's had a childhood of her own
and grows geraniums in a tin
on the wall of her project house
or steals flower bulbs from the park gardens
to grow at home
to blot out the stain of mad adults
and will not survive but thrive against all odds
as she will not let go of her own
self-belief.

ORDINARY MOTHER

(Based on a verbatim radio interview with Sue Klebold- mother of Dylan, Columbine suicide murderer)

I think I'm a normal mother
I worried, I encouraged, I coaxed, I nagged
my little boy into a big awkward teen
who banged his way downstairs into
a school mass murderer.

My Dylan, my gentle kind boy
and his patches of troubles
doing plays and sound tracks.
My sunshine boy interested in everything
a zest for life.

I held you new born and knew
a shadow, a bird of prey
crossed over us.
Sorrow held us together
in birth and death

My most important creation
my killer boy
who shot sadistically other
mothers' sunshine children
in minutes lifetimes' of love
shattered.

I read your journals too late
your secrets unfolded
each word of death new
bullets in my heart
and still They came.

Bringing food, plants,
flowers for the mother
that died that day
other sons' mothers
other ordinary mothers.

MADAME BUTTERFLIES

'the Goddess of the moon
Descends in the night
Showering all she loves
In white.'- Butterfly

Madame Butterfly was my mother.
She took me to see Butterfly
I fell in love at 8 watching her
soar in love, marry a U.S. military man
be abandoned, give birth, give away her son
and commit suicide.
I cried an orphan's tears.

Fifty years later I return
Opera North invites
our Women's Centre
to see Butterfly.
I sit among twenty women
who hardly go to theatre
eating crisps & starbursts.

Women who have been
abused, raped, violated
in & out of Care & prison
who've given up everything for love.
We wriggle slightly at the all too familiar,
Boo! at Pinkerton, scheme

sweeping butterfly off stage before
she sinks the ancestral knife inward.
They are all Madames Butterflies
crying Butterfly tears.

FROM MY MOTHER
(after Enough by Suzanne Buffam)

I learned it from my mother
who learned it from her mother before her.

How to use a knife and fork like a machine gun
to attack the food I wish I hadn't had to cook

How to be a mine field of hurt and explosive feelings
the family have to tiptoe round to arrive unsafely in bed at
night

How to prepare Christmas dinner slowly loudly banging pots
pans & cupboards until even the dog is willing to go without
its meal

How to play statues in the middle of a birthday party and
say nothing after opening all the presents

I learned it from my mother and her mother before
how to arm myself fully and carry on the war.

BLOODY MARY

I have climbed down from the altar, the stars
the golden knife sharp sun rays
and bleeding, stabbed heart sitting in my son's chest,
shudder afresh a little looking at
his bleeding head, hands, side, feet.
In some of my houses the blood bubbles
out in writhing ropes, an orgy of leaches
blood letting.

I am self-defining tonight this
Queen of Peace, this Mother of the Church
and sinners, is taking up my own chisel & paint brush
to do my own selfie or two.

My first shows me as My Boy is born.
I sit astride his bloody crown sliding out
between my legs
amidst the bright pool that held him
and an exhilarating spectrum of red tones
from baby pink to Pope magenta.

In my second….I am as it was in
the beginning of my womanhood
when I did not always have quite the right
amount of rags to catch
my monthly immaculate unconception.
From my stoney-satin folds from head to toes

over my thighs blossoms
pomegranate petals of blood
below my still composed perfect expression.

I'll take care climbing back
up above the altar
not to leave any mess.
I can't guarantee later
there will be tears of blood.

VI.   GRANDMOTHER WITCH

FALLING

My Autumn-leaved body
curling up at the edges
changing shape, colour, weight
hoping for the right moment
to let go of my grip
watching others'
unseasonable crashings

Victoria Wood, Bowie, Prince
Brexit, Trump
both your 15 year old dogs
my 15 year old cat
our end of the branch mancub
gone in a blink.
bits of me dropping
strength, pluck, buoyancy.

Shame then joy
when all grown up
I fell & broke myself
caught
by kindness and a reminder
of the bravery of vulnerability
and the finely-boned structure of
not dead yet.

How I used to crash headlong

back to mother from feral wanderings
timed to end by a fall from a tree
ripe for repair
cradling my badge of honour back home,
a physical wound gave love permission
to blossom loudly
over spilt blood
where otherwise rationed.

I am golden blood coloured
free falling
to earth
from what I've known
I stretch my fingers
arms, legs
gasp flying air
floating.

MY CROSS MOTHER

Come let me hold you
my darkling Mummy
my witch, whore mother good tit bad tit
bitch, man-eater, bastard, ball breaking
mother fucked

Come let me hold you
your scars, your bruises
your stitches, your broken bones
your insides turned out
your unhinged mind.

Come let me hold you
shaking, shivering, sighing, sobbing,
rocking, spitting, shrieking, screeching
into your own womb tomb child mother nest
of Russian dolls.

Come let me hold you
until it stops hurting
until you slowly start to mend
and sew together and look out and up
and learn to crawl, walk, play safe again.

Come let me hold you
like you didn't always hold me
because no one held you

because the mother fucked world
shut the door in your face
the doorknob just about
black eye height.

Come let me hold you
let us weep together
for the parents we wish we had
and the parent we still search for
let me hold you now like a child
before we lift you down from
The Cross.

ALLOTMENT WITCH

The rhythm of the rain and sun
kept her time as
she tried not to cut in half the worms
stirring the cauldron of the soil
clawing her way back.

She remembered last time They
had locked her out or
in, away from the garlic and onion sets,
gave her fruit trees away
her stone sets, her blue bottles.

She had broken her back nearly
wheel barrowing home her
little Eden to some other concrete
framed front
and the gate finally shut her out.

How her verdant fingers itched round
a postage stamp of lawn, a spattering
of pots but ached to dig
deeper and now she'd shape shifted her way
back in, stood spinning her fork and spade
slicing sods, unearthing the remains of the last
wyrd woman banned from sinking her
knotted hands with old mother earth.

Tripping over the rusting, ruined barrow, the pallet
the old fruit tree roots she feels the withering
of their exile and stirs more,
gulping the rain and the semaphoring
moon until the spell is unwound.

WITCH'S PULPIT

I join the hundred-plus strong crocodile
of mostly women
serpenting to the pink of St. Anne's church
on a Thursday night.
Passersby look on puzzled
more close in-
'This is the queue for…?'
We nod in sync.
soon race to the pews dodging pillars.
Five rows back I watch the whole church fill
including the double clerestory.
A choir of women doctors, lecturers
therapists and actors.
I spot the faces of familiars
packing the pews like sitting coffins,
no exit, let alone passage for the free glass
of unblessed wine
we juggle on the hymn shelf,
not wide enough to hold a book.
It's nearly an hour before she's due
and I don't mean her period.

I remember 1973, being 13, doing R.S.
the project seemed sent from above,
The Role of Women in Society.
Higher powers leapt into my life
Ariana Stassinopolis,

The Conundrum of Jan Morris and
The Female Eunuch.
What a trilogy of gender-bending
to get my young head round,
the year my body caught up with my breasts
and presented my first blood
just before Christmas
followed by raging 'glandular' fever
and my first job washing up.
The role of women in society?
75% and 25p an hour.

She is escorted to the front
to a long slow clap.
She stands at her lecterned pulpit
facing an empty aisle,
us sidled in wooden stalls, and
she cracks 'It's like a wedding.

This space is surely not designed for communicating!'
She mimics the drawl of a priest or two
bored with the sound of his own voice,
intoning as enlighteningly
as a slow-motion steam roller.
She's off…

I recall returning to Greer
after a decade of male canon
as students at a showing of

Town Bloody Hall
saw her deconstruct Norman Mailer
out of the book American Dream
my brain had been buggered with
by a young male lecturer who entering the seminar asked
'How did it make you feel, boys?'
Then, my tongue was not sharpened enough.
Later I watched her perennial appearances
in papers, journals, chat shows,
gardening and cookery book.
Surely not mainstream?
Surely not status quo?

Here she returns just in time for the new millennium
self-confessed tabloid feminist,
The Female Eunuch reincarnated
thirty years on, sixty-something.
the whole woman
no need for capitals
or inverted commas,
just in time to remind us,
even if we have fought & lost our mothers & sisters,
to remind us not to let
the multi-national, IVF,
Caesarian pushing, hysterectomy, HRT,
dieting, fetishist, fashion porn
plastic surgery
f…off developing countries with A.I.D.S.
industrial, multi-national, techno-conglomerates

cut open & suck empty
our daughters.
To love our pear-shaped, fatty-tissued,
cellulite, big-bottomed, flabby-winged
nest of our body.

And there endeth the lesson…

This is the word of a woman.

VII. WISE CRONE

G-R-O-W-L
Homage to Alan Ginsberg's HOWL

What is this noise
coming from deep within skin, muscle, bone, blood
stretching, thumping, pumping, curdling, gurgling
frothing, brothing, mewling, stewing, brewing, burning,
boiling
up and out no matter what?

Listen….to the tap tiptoeing night
crawling around the human debris
the gods of the streets sniffing
quietly the air of digital, diesel, electric drippings
those that survive and thrive, duck and dive
on a different fuel.
Left over tins, bottle dregs, unwrapped scraps,
plastic cardboard of tiny living in city trolleys
under the flyovers
under the graffitied peace sign
tents wave like flags their
soldiers stand sentry at the crossroads
cardboard signing 'everything's a blessing'.
Dollar bills slip through the car windows
for the dog, the out of work, the out of luck
at dangerous junctions in time to red, amber, gone.
a collision of fast lane burn out
and slow motion suicide.

Between the grocery and the thrift store
a hurt look, a head down, a greased crease of
taloned skin, an unclipped claw, wild coloured hair
a faithful hound, a city bindle, underneath
here lies your run away child, your abandoned wife
your take-a-chance gambling husband, your crazy Grannie
your weird uncle, your shadow self
your lost family.
Taste the tang of desert water
dripping from the rotting veg & fruit
watch the Goodwill worker let the dog friend in
turn a blind eye to the unpaid for hat that walks out
see the tattooed eyed young woman drag the
bed box of clothes behind her and hound
to sit on the sidewalk unpicking stitches.

Touch this shoulder lightly
hold my dying hand
dance with me one more time before I can't
reach me, remind me what a kiss tastes like
how a tickle laughs, how a third arm can embrace
like a wing.
Fly with my tangled mind
my complicated, tattered monkish life
march with my street saints
I'll sing for a dollar
take my pic for a few coins
zoom in your long lens look
'what can I give you…'

poor as we are- this
broken homed, broken hearted
broken down
growl of an animal?

EL CORAZON DE MEXICO

We tour the Mercado knick knacks
stalls of tin art, milagroes
hearts red plum on fire & bursting
into flaming swords and wings
retablos, skeletons, day of the dead
dancing their bones through
every milestone of life.
Remember the moments
that made you feel alive
flashing before your eyes.

You alert us on our travels to you,
an arrhythmic heart event
coffee, exhaustion, eldering, old smoking.
We taxi race with you to Queretaro
through a heart stopping wacky races
round u-turns, one ways, fly overs,
truck accident, road works, tolls
5 minutes before the appointment-
Institute of The Heart
logo a heart within a heart within a heart.
In the waiting room all
our hearts pump louder to the wait
the flat screen on the wall shows
old episodes of Gray's Anatomy-a
cardiac resuscitation.

Only one of us can go with you
to the heart consultant
gown on front open laid down
jellied & hooked up to a screen
I tick between light & heavy hearted
'I can confirm it's not a baby' I blurt.
The shock of seeing a four chambered pump
hearing the squish & squash of life
'where are the flames, the daggers, the wings?'

Heart halter on and monitoring
we tour Queretaro then home to
cobbled streets at a more even evening pace.
Doctor has dared you to be 'bad' to
test your heart on a beer, a coffee, steps.
We are counting down our 10 day
visit together, the town sign, crest
carvings finally catches my eye
San Miguel de Allende
The Heart of Mexico.

THE HOUSE OF MEMORIES
(painting by Claudia Williams)

She is held by his big hands at the end
of his heavy overcoat framing
a stony face beneath his flat cap.
Their lives' things are tugged at
strained, boxed and clutched
out of the gaping front door.

Unmoved men move the hall mirror that saw
dozens of friends pass by.
The elder girl hugs the old sewing machine
that thread together her own clothes
that would keep young bones warm until they
stretched beyond her reach.
The bulb is bare now below the bedroom
she lie in with him a thousand nights
through sickness and health of
babies' sickly, gurgling, toddlings and parental catchings.
The gate has been removed for the removing.
She holds her chin over the knot
of her headscarf
holds onto the family portrait in her other
holds it all, holds her breath and looks

FIRST HAND, LAST HAND

The first hand held was
Mother's
who first stroked us, fed us, cleaned us, dressed us,
whose finger led us along a line of words
worked her fingers to the bone for us
admonished & applauded us
tipped us hard saved pocket money
hoorayed us onto schools, college, & jobs
tugged us through teen tantrums
looking back at the uppish girl she once was
like her mother & her mother before did
hugged us through break ups and make ups
lovers lost and found
enjoyed our pets like our children
and never tired of holding us or being held
always happy for more of our company.

Time's hands tic-tocs her
back to a daughter's hands
returning the favours
helping her dress, reading to her,
buying her the treats she will not buy herself
mildly mocking her set ways we will adopt
loving her pets like grandchildren too
holding her ever more carefully
to keep her paper skin bruise free
helping her brittle bones to keep walking

& eating the last few enjoyables

And if we are very lucky
finally holding her like the child we were
waving to other mothers in the sky
on the last great goodbye
the first hand we held
the last hand she holds
in unconditional, blameless
everlasting acceptance and love
Our mother.

WHEN WOMEN FLY: REVIEW

"In our world where women are still often reduced to how they look or what they can do for others, rather than who they are, a book like this is not just a powerful and beautiful work of art, it's a necessary one. With nods to well-known women real and fictional, from Virginia Woolf to Madame Butterfly, and drawing much from real lived experiences, Sarah Pritchard not only shows us what happens 'When women fly...', but what happens when they fall, and everything in between."

Kate Garrett, poet & editor

ACKNOWLEDGEMENTS

Thanks to the following presses who have had the courage & freedom to publish versions of these poems

SKIN BETRAYED
Degenerate Voices on Domestic Violence 2017

PRIVATE NAMES
Central Library Touring Poetry Exhibition 1996

FAIRY GODDAUGHTER
The Grapple Annual No.2 (awaiting publication date)

NOT A GIRL YET
Prong & Posy   2016

HOW DARE YOU & BREAST
Beyond Paradise, Crocus 1990

THE LESBIAN IN US
Noble Dissenters, Beautiful Dragons 2017

CHEMICAL SUN SET
Manchester Poets 3 Puppy Wolf Press 2012

DEAR VIRGINIA
Deranged, Picaroon 2017

NAMING ME
Nailing Colours: poems of rebellion Crocus1997

WINTER BEACH
Cahoots 1993
ORDINARY MOTHER
Bang 2017

I LEARNED IT FROM MY MOTHER
Degenerates June 2017

ALLOTMENT WITCH
Full Moon & Foxglove Three Drops Press 2016

G-R-O-W-L
One Person's Trash   2017

EL CORAZON DE MEXICO
Bonnie's Crew: poems helping hearts of all ages 2018

HOUSE OF MEMORIES
Silver Birch 2016

GUITAR WOMAN
Sinister Wisdon 2020

STIRRED ZINES: STIRRED PRESS 2015-7:

WHEN I DRINK YOU
Desire

OMNILOVE
Bjork

SKELETON TREE
Winter

GRASSROOTS
Women Beats

FALLING
A Forest

ALSO BY SARAH PRITCHARD

AFTER THE FLOOD

30 poems in 30 days for National Poetry Writing Month
NaPoWriMo

Shortlisted chapbook 2017 by Local Gems Press, published
2018. Theme: 1953 flood of East Anglia, where Sarah comes
from.

You picked him up from the beach
his cowboy hat caught
in his swollen neck.
limp as a drowned fish
you carried him back to land
and continued your duty.

***

Rex scratched at his Dad's face
to wake them.

Her pony swam behind
the little girl in a boat.

***

When the wind is silent
when the birds come back
when the birds sing
we know it is safe again.

After the Flood depicts the incidents and aftermath of a flood in 1953. The sea is instantly characterised as a destructive force, the coastal erosion of the Norfolk Coast humanised by many view points on a storm. We are given detailed images of the destruction " A trail of babies' bottles/spectacles and false teeth.". Real life is rendered surreal "shrieking, swimming pigs." The land is overtaken by the sea. The poems effectively give the sense of an unprepared community experiencing something unprecedented.

Anna Percy

With powerful observation and stunning twists and turns of language **After The Flood** captures all the tumult, horror, and strange wonder of the event and its aftermath. Pritchard's writing mirrors the terrific pace of the tidal surge itself and whirls us through to land – safely – in a tree of birds just starting to sing again.

Char March

Sarah Pritchard

Sarah60pegasus@gmail.com
Facebook: english alien

HIDDEN VOICE PUBLISHING

Hidden Voice Publishing is an independent publishing resource centre that supports & represents authors from under-represented groups with publishing paperback and Amazon Kindle books.

TITLES ON HIDDEN VOICE PUBLISHING

I KNOW WHY THE GAY MAN DANCES
JOEL SADLER-PUCKERING

INKY BLACK WOMAN
MINA AIDOO

FERAL ANIMALS
JOEL SADLER-PUCKERING

WHEN WOMEN FLY
SARAH PRITCHARD

HIDDEN VOICE 2019 ANTHOLOGY
VARIOUS AUTHORS
(OUT SUMMER 2019)

Printed in Poland
by Amazon Fulfillment
Poland Sp. z o.o., Wrocław

49709885R00068